WORLD WATCH

WORLD HEALTH ORGANIZATION

Cath Senker

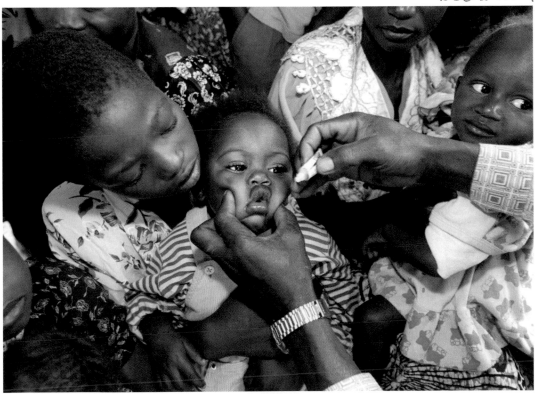

HODDER
Wayland

an imprint of Hodder Children's Books

WORLDWATCH SERIES

Greenpeace • Red Cross • UNICEF • United Nations • World Health Organization • WWF

Produced for Hodder Wayland by White-Thomson Publishing Ltd,
2/3 St Andrew's Place, Lewes, East Sussex BN7 1UP

© 2003 White-Thomson Publishing

Published in Great Britain in 2003 by Hodder Wayland, an imprint of Hodder Children's Books.

Project editor: Nicola Edwards
Commissioning editor: Steve White-Thomson
Proofreader and indexer: Alison Cooper
Design: Jane Hawkins
Picture research: Shelley Noronha, Glass Onion Pictures

British Library Cataloguing in Publication data
Senker, Cath
   WHO – (Worldwatch)
   1. World Health Organization - Juvenile literature
   I. Title II. Edwards, Nicola
   362.1'0601
ISBN 0 7502 4334 1

Printed in Hong Kong
Hodder Children's Books, a division of Hodder Headline Limited, 338 Euston Road, London NW1 3BH.

Picture acknowledgements: Cover ©GiacomoPirozzi/Panos Pictures; title page WHO; p4 Popperfoto, Reuters/RTV; p5 Popperfoto, Reuters Uganda Out; p6 Popperfoto, Reuters; p8 WHO/Sven Torfinn; p11 WHO/Pierre Virot; p12 ©Giacomo Pirozzi/Panos Pictures; p13 WHO; p14 Topham; p15 Popperfoto, Ian Hodgson/Reuters; p16 ©Hartmut Schwarzbach/Still Pictures; p17 WHO/PAHO/AMRO; p18 Mark Edwards/Still Pictures; p19 Mark Edwards/Still Pictures; p20 WHO/Pierre Virot; p21 Paul Harrison/Still Pictures; p22 ©Giacomo Pirozzi/Panos Pictures; p23 Topham Picturepoint; p24 Still Pictures; p25 Exile Images; p26 Popperfoto, Reuters; p27 ©Giacomo Pirozzi/Panos Pictures; p28 WHO; p29 Popperfoto, Reuters; p30 Popperfoto, Mike Hutchings/Reuters; p31 WHO/Pierre Virot; p32 Popperfoto, Darren Whiteside/Reuters; p33 WHO; p34 H. Davies/Exile Images; pp36/37 Salim Amin/Camerapix; p38 Popperfoto, Will Burgess/Reuters; p39 Popperfoto, Zainal Abd Halim/Reuters; p40 Paul Harrison/Still Pictures; p41 © WHO/OMS; p42 ©Sean Sprague/Panos Pictures; p43 Mark Edwards/Still Pictures; p44 Topham/Image Works; p45 Ron Giling/Still Pictures.

Cover: A child drinking safe, clean water.

CONTENTS

Chapter One:
WHO Takes Action   **4**

Chapter Two:
The History, Structure and Aims of WHO   **6**

Chapter Three:
The Campaign Against Disease   **16**

Chapter Four:
Promoting Better Health   **22**

Chapter Five:
On the Frontline: Disease Control   **28**

Chapter Six:
On the Frontline: Health Promotion   **34**

Chapter Seven:
Successes and Challenges   **40**

Glossary   **46**

Further Information   **47**

Index   **48**

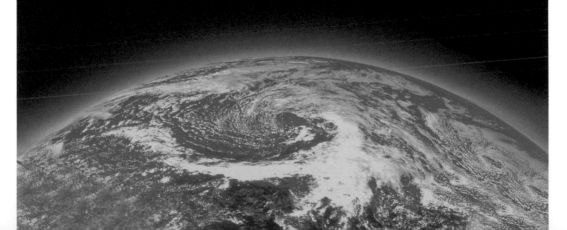

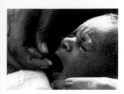

Chapter One:
WHO Takes Action

EBOLA EMERGENCY!

16 October 2000, Kampala. At the meeting at the World Health Organization (WHO) office in Kampala, Uganda, things were tense. 'We've got 71 suspected cases and 35 people have already died,' said one of the officers. 'We've never seen Ebola in Uganda before – we have to act quickly before this turns into a disaster.'

Ebola fever is a virus, one of the most deadly known to humankind, causing death in 50 to 90 per cent of all cases.

Just a week earlier, on 8 October, the first reports of an unusual illness with fever had reached the Ugandan Ministry of Health. The first person to identify the outbreak of the disease in a local hospital in Gulu district was Dr Matthew Lukwiya. As soon as he alerted the health ministry, they rushed off samples to a lab in South Africa for identification. Without even waiting for the results, the government gave WHO and its partners access to the outbreak area.

Bad news confirmed

The terrible news came back from the lab that it was indeed Ebola. Experts in disease control from the WHO headquarters in Geneva, Switzerland, jumped on a plane to Kampala to offer their assistance.

WHO and its partners in the Global Outbreak Alert and Response Network (an international partnership of institutions that pool their resources to respond to outbreaks of disease) put emergency plans into action to prevent the disease from spreading. Suspected cases were kept separate from other patients. All hospital staff members were briefed about the dangers. They were told to use strict barrier nursing techniques. This meant it was vital to wear their own individual gowns, gloves and masks, rather than sharing them.

Medical workers help a patient with the Ebola virus during the outbreak of October 2000 in Uganda. ▼

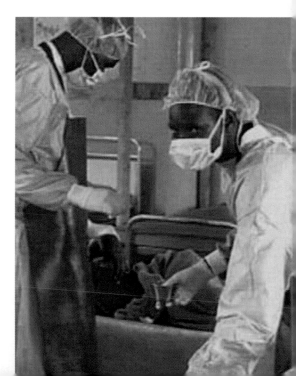

Community alert

In the community, measures to control the disease were rapidly put into place. People who had had close contact with a patient with Ebola were kept under strict supervision. Anyone with a fever above 38.3°C was sent to hospital immediately and put in strict isolation.

By the end of February 2001, the outbreak of Ebola was officially over. It had killed 224 people, including Dr Lukwiya and other health workers. More than 20 international organizations from the Global Outbreak Alert and Response Network, including WHO, had worked together to combat the Ebola outbreak.

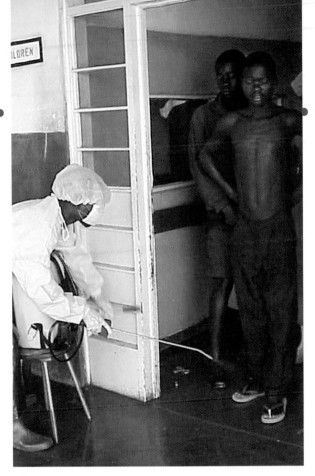

▲ A health worker during the Ebola outbreak spraying people suspected of having the virus, in Gulu hospital.

ORGANIZATION IN FOCUS:
WHO takes action

Whenever there is a major natural disaster or war, WHO is key to the relief operation. For example, if there is a hurricane, earthquake or volcanic eruption, a WHO task force will be on the scene within 48 hours to help to assess health problems. Task force members will help to control diseases, such as cholera, that can spread when thousands are left homeless and without safe water supplies and sanitation facilities. WHO also co-ordinates efforts to bring international aid to the emergency zone.

In the nineteenth century, Europe was overrun by an outbreak of cholera, a deadly infectious disease. It was spread through people sharing dirty water supplies. An international conference was held to talk about how to tackle communicable diseases – such as cholera and smallpox – which can be passed from one person to another. In 1851, representatives from 12 countries met in Paris, France. They discussed sanitation measures to keep places clean and remove human waste but failed to reach an agreement.

In 1892, the European countries adopted the International Sanitary Convention to try to deal with cholera. Ten years later, the International Sanitary Bureau was set up in Washington DC, USA. A public health office was established in Paris in 1907, with senior public health officials from twelve member states, nine of them European.

INTERNATIONAL CO-OPERATION

The idea of developing international organizations to cope with worldwide problems was given a boost after the catastrophe of the First World War. The League of Nations was set up mainly to try to prevent another war. One of the organization's additional tasks was to prevent and control disease. To this end the Health Organization of the League of Nations was created in 1919.

There was some progress in the 1920s and 1930s. For example, the International Sanitary Convention was updated in 1926 to include measures to control smallpox and typhus, which were common at the time.

◀ These children in India are holding placards with health messages during a rally to mark World Health Day.

THE BIRTH OF WHO

In 1939 the Second World War began. Afterwards, once more, there were determined attempts to build institutions to prevent future conflict. The United Nations was established in 1945 and a new health organization was proposed. The World Health Organization came into being on 7 April 1948 – this day is now celebrated as World Health Day each year. By the time the first World Health Assembly was held in June, 53 governments had become members of WHO. In 2002 there were 191 member countries.

"Health is a state of complete physical, mental and social well-being and not merely the absence of disease or infirmity."

The WHO definition of health

ORGANIZATION IN FOCUS:
The aim of WHO

The aim of WHO is the 'attainment by all peoples of the highest possible level of health'. It has responsibilities to:

• help governments to improve their health services

• collect and store information about health issues

• help to eradicate all types of disease

• promote better housing, sanitation and working conditions

• encourage scientists and professionals to work together to improve health

• propose international agreements on health matters

• carry out research into health issues

• develop international standards for food and medicine

• help to improve health education.

▲ A baby in Congo being given a drop containing the Oral Polio Vaccine. The drop contains a very weak form of the disease. The baby's body will produce antibodies to fight it. If he ever comes into contact with the polio virus, his body will already possess the antibodies with which to combat it.

A HISTORY OF HEALTH CAMPAIGNS

Since its establishment in 1948, WHO has run a series of major health campaigns focusing on immunization as a means of preventing dangerous communicable diseases.

In 1974, WHO launched an Expanded Programme on Immunization (EPI) to protect children from poliomyelitis (polio), measles, diphtheria, whooping cough, tetanus and tuberculosis. These diseases had a serious effect on the health of the world's children. It was an 'expanded' programme because new vaccines against polio and measles had been added. In addition, immunization was now to become more widespread. Incredibly, only 5 per cent of children were being vaccinated in developing countries (the poorer countries that are trying to advance their industry and economic system).

In poorer countries with few resources, it was difficult to raise the rate of children immunized against these six dangerous diseases. Between 1974 and 1980, WHO worked with other organizations, such as the United Nations Children's Fund (UNICEF), to develop training materials. Hundreds of training courses were held to help local health workers to spread the programme more widely. By 1998 the global figure for children vaccinated under the EPI had reached 80 per cent.

A GLOBAL AIDS STRATEGY

In 1987 WHO launched its Global Programme on AIDS. AIDS is spread through HIV (the human immunodeficiency virus). In most people, the virus slowly destroys their immune system so that they are prone to infection and catch diseases easily. AIDS is the last stage of HIV infection and leads to death.

AIDS spread relentlessly throughout the 1980s and 1990s. It had a devastating impact on people's lives and affected the development of entire countries. By the end of 1996, there had been more than 8 million cases worldwide, resulting in 6 million deaths. More than 90 per cent of infections occurred in developing countries. WHO and six other organizations banded together in 1996 to form UNAIDS, which aimed to prevent the spread of AIDS and to help people affected by it.

FACTFILE: Milestones in WHO's history

1948 WHO is founded.

1948 A single penicillin injection is introduced to cure yaws, an infectious tropical skin disease causing large red swellings.

1974 Expanded Programme on Immunization is introduced.

1980 Global Commission states that smallpox has been eradicated worldwide.

1987 Global Programme on AIDS is introduced.

1998 Fiftieth anniversary of the signing of the WHO Constitution.

2002 The eradication of polio is declared in Europe.

ORGANIZATION IN FOCUS:
WHO – how it works

THE WORLD HEALTH ASSEMBLY (WHA)

Every year, representatives from all the member states and from international health organizations go to Geneva, Switzerland for a meeting. Here, the representatives decide what WHO will do over the next two years – and how they will spend their budget. At the 2002 meeting, there were discussions on risks to health and how to reduce them. The budget for that year was almost US $400 million.

The WHA also appoints the director-general, for one or two five-year terms. He or she leads WHO.

THE EXECUTIVE BOARD

The board is made up of 32 health experts from different member states. It puts into practice what has been decided at the WHA. It also decides on emergency measures to deal with disasters or outbreaks of disease.

REGIONAL OFFICES

The member states of WHO are divided into six regions and each has a regional office. The regional offices are Africa, the Americas, South-east Asia, Europe, the Eastern Mediterranean and the Western Pacific. Every regional office is responsible for the work in that region and sends out experts and field workers to individual countries.

THE SECRETARIAT

The secretariat is the staff of the organization. There are about 3,500 staff members worldwide, from medical and health experts to chemists, translators and accountants.

HOW WHO WORKS

The World Health Organization is part of the United Nations, an organization made up of all the countries in the world that aims to keep world peace.

Partners

WHO works with many organizations in the United Nations system such as the World Bank and other financial institutions. It also works with regional organizations, such as the European Union and the Organization of American States. Non-governmental organizations (NGOs), such as Oxfam, are also involved; 189 international NGOs have official relations with WHO.

Funding

WHO receives money contributed by its member nations, depending on their wealth and population. The richest countries – the USA, Japan, Germany, France and Britain – give the most. WHO also receives voluntary donations from governments for specific programmes and to help cope with emergencies. Private companies donate goods, such as vaccines, and some individuals make personal donations.

The Director-General of WHO has a high profile. Here, Dr Gro Harlem Brundtland (centre) is visiting a village in Nigeria, on African Malaria Day. ▼

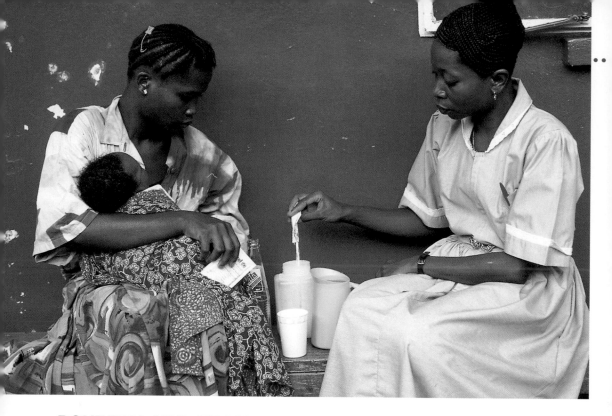

POVERTY AND HEALTH

In 1999 in a hospital in Niger, one of the poorest countries of the world, a little girl called Zenibou died. She was weak from malaria but her mother didn't have enough money to pay for her treatment. Zenibou's mother left the hospital with the body of her dead daughter on her back.

The link between ill-health and poverty is now widely understood. Today, 600 million children – a quarter of the world's child population – live in families that survive on less than US $1 a day. They do not have enough food and don't have access to clean water. This makes them weak, so they tend to fall ill.

THE COST OF A CURE

Thousands of people daily are dying needlessly from diseases that could be prevented. In poor countries, 30,000

▲ A nurse in Sierra Leone shows a mother how to mix oral rehydration salts with clean water.

people die each day because effective medicines are too expensive or not available. Many children in those countries die from conditions such as diarrhoea. Diarrhoea is common where people do not have access to clean water – which is the case for one-third of the world's children. The illness can easily be treated with basic rehydration salts, which replace the essential elements the body needs, but many people cannot get them.

Zenibou, for instance, would have lived if her mother could have afforded to pay for her treatment. Alternatively, if Niger were not such a poor country, spending most of its income on repaying debt, there would be more money to spend on health services.

WHO's mission is to tackle the key global issue of world health. It faces huge challenges in bringing good health to the world. For example, WHO works with the pharmaceutical (drug) industry to find cures for diseases. But the companies will only produce new drugs if they can make a large profit. This is why drugs are often too expensive for poor

▲ A child drinking clean water. WHO research shows that about 1.7 million deaths a year are caused by unsafe water, and poor sanitation and hygiene. Most of these deaths are of children.

countries to buy. Therefore WHO, and all those who work towards world health, face an uphill struggle.

FACTFILE: The global health divide

- In 2000, 11 million children under 5 died – 97% of them in developing countries.
- Vaccines can prevent death yet 777,000 children die each year from measles, mostly in developing and least developed countries.
- During a period of 10 years between 1990 and 2000, life expectancy of over a billion people has gone down by 10 years from 50 to 40.

Source: Médecins Sans Frontières

UNHEALTHY LIVING

Poverty is not the only cause of disease. There are serious risks to human health from environmental causes and social problems. The way people eat, drink and smoke is of worldwide concern. According to WHO, nearly 60 per cent of deaths globally are due to non-communicable diseases (ones that cannot be caught from another person) such as heart disease, stroke, cancer and lung disease.

This woman is wearing a nicotine patch to help her to stop smoking. ▼

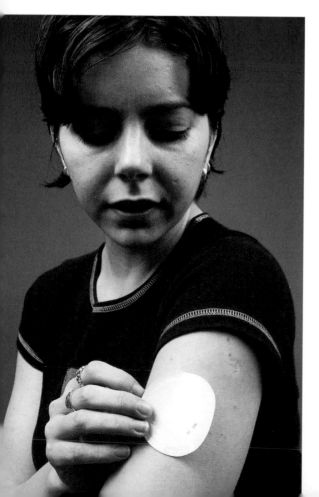

BAD HABITS

Across the world, 4 million people are killed by their smoking habit each year. Young people in Europe, especially girls, are now smoking more than their parents have ever done. Obesity is a new area of great concern. Increasing numbers of people, especially in the developed world, do jobs that involve little physical activity. Even in their leisure time they may not do much exercise. Growing numbers of people are obese – so fat that it is dangerous for their health. Obese people are at higher risk from serious conditions, such as heart disease and diabetes.

Drinking too much alcohol is a worldwide problem – 140 million people in the world are dependent on alcohol. In Europe, one in four deaths of men aged 15 to 29 is related to drunkenness. Under the influence of alcohol people cause traffic accidents and commit violent crimes.

FOOD SAFETY SCARES

Food safety is a major challenge. For the majority of the world's people, simply getting enough to eat is difficult. Those in rich countries may get enough to eat but what about the quality of the food? The Western world has been rocked by scandals. For example, it was realized in Britain in 1986 that poor farming practices had caused BSE, a fatal disease in cattle that could be passed on to humans.

RICH WORLD, POOR WORLD

WHO aims to help people all over the world to live more healthily. It has to try to keep a balance – and be seen to keep a balance – between dealing with 'rich world' and 'poor world' health problems. There is a feeling on the part of the poor that there has been greater readiness to deal with conditions such as obesity, smoking, cancer and stress. Less attention has been paid to tackling diseases such as malaria. It is simply more profitable for pharmaceutical companies to invest in cures for 'rich world' problems because wealthier countries can more easily afford the cost of their drugs.

> **"**The world is living dangerously: either because it has little choice, or because it is making the wrong choices about consumption and activity.**"**
>
> Director-General of WHO, Dr Gro Harlem Brundtland, May 2002

In Britain in 2000, millions of animals, like this unfortunate cow, were sent to slaughter in an attempt to stop the deadly disease BSE from spreading further. ▼

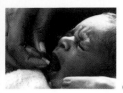

Chapter Three:
The Campaign Against Disease

Stamping out communicable diseases that cause disability and death is one of WHO's most important tasks. Since 1974, the Expanded Programme on Immunization has been used to control dangerous infectious diseases.

MEASLES

Measles can be a very serious illness. Up to one in twenty children who catch it will get pneunomia. About one child in every 1,000 will get encephalitis, a brain disease that can leave a child deaf or with a learning disability. Of every 1,000 children who get measles, one or two will die from it.

Many countries have successfully reduced cases of measles. Mass immunization campaigns in the Americas have meant that measles has virtually disappeared from the two continents. But thousands of cases continue to occur in many of the larger developing countries, especially in Africa. In densely populated areas, the disease spreads quickly.

ESSENTIAL DRUGS – A HUMAN RIGHT?

Hepatitis B is a liver disease that can cause lifelong infection and death. A vaccine for hepatitis B became available in the early 1980s but it was so expensive that only a few countries could afford it. When manufacturers began to compete with each other to produce and sell the hepatitis B vaccine the price fell dramatically. By 1998 the vaccine had been introduced into 100 countries compared to only 20 in 1990.

The cost of vaccines is a general problem for poor countries. WHO runs a campaign to persuade pharmaceutical companies to offer essential medicines, such as vaccines, at reduced prices for developing countries. The organization argues

This hepatitis sufferer is being treated by a nurse in Germany. Many sufferers in African countries do not have access to treatment available in developed nations. ▼

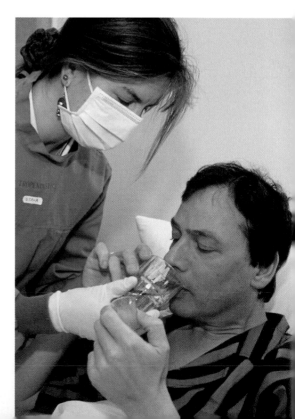

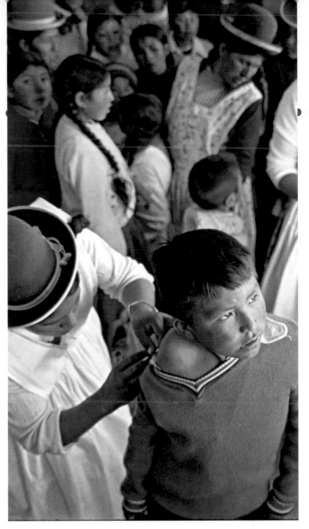

A child in Bolivia being vaccinated against measles, part of the mass campaign in the South American continent to eradicate the disease. ▶

that access to essential drugs is a human right and that they should not be just another product to be traded. But there are many things stopping this work from being effective. For example, pharmaceutical companies insist they have to charge a high price in order to pay for the huge costs of research and development of their drugs. They put a patent on them, which also keeps the price high (see factfile).

FACTFILE: Patents

A patent is the sole right to make or use an invention for a certain length of time. Companies take out patents so that they can profit from all the work they have put into developing a product, without it being copied. Transnational drug companies (companies that work in many different countries) hold more than 90 per cent of drugs patents. Patents keep the cost of drugs high because there is no competition from other companies to bring the prices down.

The Trade Related Aspects of Intellectual Property Rights agreement (TRIPS), due to be introduced by all countries by 2006, will allow at least 20 years' patent protection on all forms of products, including drugs.

Source: Oxfam

THE KILLER AIDS

Twenty years after the first case of AIDS was reported, it has become one of the most devastating diseases humankind has ever faced. AIDS is now the leading cause of death in sub-Saharan Africa. Worldwide, it is the fourth biggest killer. At the end of 2002, about 42 million people in the world were living with HIV.

In many developing countries, the majority of new infections occur in young adults. Young women are particularly likely to become infected. About one-third of those currently living with HIV/AIDS are aged between 15 and 24. Most of them do not even realize that they are carrying the virus.

UNAIDS

WHO has been helping to tackle AIDS through the UNAIDS programme since 1996. UNAIDS co-ordinates action against AIDS.

▲ 'Miss Universe 1999' Mpule Kwelegobe (centre) is a Goodwill Ambassador for the UN Population Fund. Here she discusses AIDS with teenage mothers in Botswana.

In developing countries it supports the organizations that are dealing with the disease. WHO is involved in monitoring the spread of AIDS and keeping statistics. It also offers guidance on the care, treatment and support of people with AIDS. Another vital strand is working with the International Federation of Pharmaceutical Manufacturers to research and develop new drugs to stop the virus.

CHEAP GENERICS

Nowadays there are medicines available that can keep people with AIDS alive, but they are very expensive. The high price puts treatment out of poor people's reach.

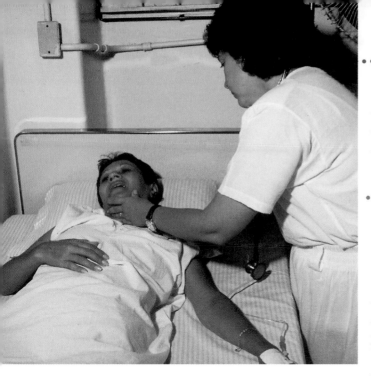

An AIDS patient in Brazil is given drugs free of charge. Such access to AIDS drugs has helped many thousands of Brazilians.

LITTLE PROVISION FOR THE POOR

Since 2000, UNAIDS has run a programme to supply AIDS drugs at a reduced price to African countries – but apparently the drugs are still not cheap enough. A UNAIDS report in 2002 revealed the scandalous fact that only 30,000 people out of the almost 30 million living with HIV/AIDS in sub-Saharan Africa were being given the drugs they needed to keep them alive. Unless affordable treatment can be provided, the future for the millions living with the death sentence of HIV/AIDS looks bleak indeed.

Some countries have companies that produce low-cost generic drugs. These are drugs that have no brand name and are not protected by a patent. For example, Brazil produces its own cheap generic AIDS drugs. Since 1996 it has provided these drugs free of charge to Brazilians with HIV/AIDS. But the TRIPS agreement (see page 17) threatens such schemes.

FACTFILE: HIV/AIDS

- In Botswana in 2002, almost 40 per cent of adults were HIV positive. Among pregnant women aged 25 to 29, 55.6 per cent had the virus.

  Source: UNAIDS report, 2002

- The Indian generic drugs company Cipla offers its AIDS treatment for US$150–300 per year per patient. The patented version costs US$10,000–15,000 per year.

  Source: Third World Network, 2001

TROPICAL DISEASES

Each year millions of people die from tropical diseases, while conditions such as leprosy leave thousands disabled. WHO is campaigning actively to try to stamp out these diseases.

Curing leprosy

Leprosy is still a problem in 24 African, Asian and Latin American countries. It comes from a kind of bacterium (a tiny form of life that can cause disease) and destroys flesh – permanently. Throughout history, people afflicted by it have been cut off by their communities and forced to live separately. Recent efforts to control leprosy have been successful. In 1981 multi-drug therapy (MDT) was recommended by a WHO Study Group. It kills the disease and cures the patient. The pharmaceutical companies Novartis and the Novartis Foundation for Sustainable Development made MDT available free of charge for all leprosy patients. WHO ensured that sufficient quantities of the drug were provided to countries with a leprosy problem.

Blinded by blackfly

River blindness (onchocerciasis) is the world's second leading infectious cause of blindness. This terrible disease is spread by blackflies that live on fast-flowing rivers, mostly in sub-Saharan African countries. The Onchocerciasis Control Programme (OCP) was launched in 1974 by WHO and other organizations, including the World Bank. The main method of controlling the disease has been to use insecticides to kill the

A former leprosy sufferer in Ethiopia. By 2002, WHO member states had achieved their target to decrease the level of leprosy in the world by over 90 per cent. ▼

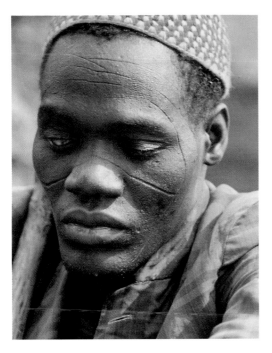

▲ The blackfly carries tiny worms, which get into the human body and produce tiny larvae. The larvae cause rashes, itching and muscle pain. They attack the eyes, leading to blindness.

blackfly. People who have the disease can take a drug called Mectizan ® to kill the worms.

Mosquitoes and malaria

Today, 40 per cent of the world's population, mostly in the poorest countries, are at risk of malaria. Sub-Saharan African countries are the worst affected. Malaria is spread by mosquitoes carrying the malaria parasite when they bite people.

It causes fever, headaches and vomiting, and can become life-threatening if not treated promptly. Drugs have been produced to treat it, but the malaria parasites have become resistant to one drug after another, meaning that new drugs have to be developed all the time. One of the best strategies is to prevent people from being bitten by mosquitoes in the first place (see pages 28 and 29).

FACTFILE: Achievements of the OCP programme

- In 1974, more than 1 million people in West Africa suffered from river blindness. Of these, 100,000 had serious eye problems and 35,000 were blind. By 2000, there were hardly any infected people in the seven countries where the programme was originally launched.
- The drug Mectizan ® is donated free by the pharmaceutical company Merck, Sharp & Dohme. The cost of distributing Mectizan ® tablets to a whole community is just 50p per person per year.
- Malaria kills an African child every 30 seconds.

Chapter Four:
Promoting Better Health

In 1977, the World Health Assembly decided that a major goal of WHO and member governments should be 'Health for All'. Everyone was to have access to health care and people were to be taught how to prevent illness.

ENCOURAGING HEALTHY CHOICES

WHO promotes campaigns to help people to make healthy choices in their lives, such as eating a good diet. Getting the message across to young people is vital. In 1995 WHO launched the Global School Health Initiative to help schools to become health-promoting institutions. The aim was to encourage healthy habits and prevent disease among students and the school community. This included providing wholesome food, plenty of opportunities for physical exercise, and counselling for people with problems. The policy has been adopted by schools around the globe.

HEALTH IN THE SUNSHINE

WHO's Global UV Project, part of its Global School Health Initiative, looked at sun protection. The project's aim is to change children's attitudes and behaviour, encouraging them to cover up, wear a hat and use sun cream.

To make it easier to judge when protection is needed, WHO and other organizations have produced a Global Solar UV Index. It is a measure of UV radiation at the Earth's surface. Along with the weather forecast, people can find out how dangerous the sun's rays will be that day and protect their skin in a sensible way.

◀ Girls in this Kenyan school learn about the importance of good nutrition in their cookery classes.

NO CHOICE IN THE MATTER

However, 'Health for All' is hard to achieve in countries too poor to provide good health care and where people are too poor to choose healthy options – even if they know about them. In many developing countries, people do not get enough to eat. Many others worldwide eat the wrong foods because they are cheaper. In Buenos Aires, Argentina, a survey in 2002 noted that the prices of fresh fruit, vegetables, lean meats and milk products tended to increase more than the prices of other goods. It was cheaper for people to fill themselves up with unhealthy foods rich in carbohydrates, fats and sugars. The economic situation means that WHO has had little success in this area.

▲ These children in China have to put their health at risk by walking to school through dense pollution.

"The poor do not eat what they want, nor what they know that they should eat, but what they can get."

Patricia Aguirre of Argentina's Ministry of Health and Social Action, 2002

FACTFILE: Environmental problems and children

According to WHO, almost one-third of the burden of disease in the world is because of environmental risks, including malnutrition and a lack of clean water. Over 40% of this burden falls on children under 5 years of age, even though they account for only 10% of the world's population.

23

LIFE AND DEATH IN PREGNANCY AND CHILDHOOD

Each year, nearly 600,000 women die from pregnancy-related causes. An astonishing 99 per cent of these deaths occur in less developed countries.

WHO developed the Making Pregnancy Safer (MPS) strategy in 2000. It aims to ensure that women have a skilled birth attendant to look after them before, during and after birth, and access to other health care that they need. The initiative has been introduced in ten 'spotlight' countries.

A woman works in the fields, in the Altiplano region of Bolivia. More than three times as many mothers die in childbirth in the Altiplano area than in urban areas of Bolivia. ▼

Poverty and pregnancy

One of these countries is Bolivia. The problem of high maternal death rates is particularly acute in the Altiplano area. It is mostly made up of isolated villages inhabited by indigenous (native) peoples with their own traditions and culture. Extremely poor and generally uneducated, the women have little to do with the official health services. Seventy per cent give birth at home. If things go wrong, the results can be fatal. A key aim of the MPS strategy in Bolivia is to make the health service sensitive to the culture of indigenous people so that they feel comfortable coming to use the facilities. The Bolivian Ministry of Health has now adopted WHO's guidelines for managing problems in pregnancy and childbirth.

Disease increases the danger

Disease makes pregnancy and childbirth more dangerous. For instance, AIDS has become just as common among women as men. Mothers can pass on the virus to their babies.

"How can I take care [of myself]? I'm always working, picking rice and pulses, digging pits and fetching water. I was in the fields until two hours before my baby was born."

Mangala, India, who gave birth to a premature (early) baby with a low birth weight.

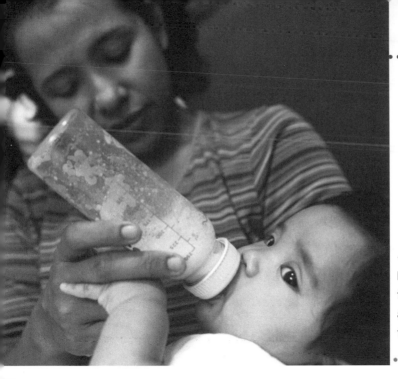

◀ An exception to the breastfeeding policy: bottle feeding by mothers with HIV avoids passing on the virus to the baby.

Malaria is particularly harmful during pregnancy. Yet when spotted, it can be treated to avoid the death of both mother and child.

BREASTFEEDING IS BEST

If children are not properly fed in the first few years of their lives, they will die. Malnutrition is the underlying cause of 60 per cent of child deaths. According to WHO research, in most cases it is best if mothers breastfeed their babies, and do not give them any other foods, until they are six months old. In 1992, WHO and UNICEF launched the Baby-friendly Hospital Initiative. The aim was to encourage mothers to breastfeed from the moment their baby was born. The initiative had been implemented in about 16,000 hospitals in 171 countries by 2000. It has helped to increase the rates of breastfeeding throughout the world.

FACTFILE: Deaths of mothers and babies

Women from the world's poorest households (with an income of less than US$1 a day) are at least 300 times more likely to die due to pregnancy or childbirth-related causes than those who are better off. Some 3.9 million babies a year are stillborn (born dead). In addition, about 3 million newborn babies die within the first week of life.

Source: Department of Reproductive Health and Research (RHR), WHO, 2001

MENTAL HEALTH

Mental health problems affect about a quarter of people at some point in their lives. In 2001, WHO made mental health the subject of its annual report in an effort to raise awareness of mental health problems. This is a growing area of concern in the world today. Mental health is just as important as physical health to people's well-being. People who are anxious and depressed are more likely to develop physical diseases too. Also, they are more likely to behave in ways that are bad for their health, for example, drinking unsafe amounts of alcohol and smoking.

Tension and depression

Depression is one of the biggest health problems in society and the problem is set to get worse. This is not just an issue in wealthy countries where people get enough to eat and have time to ponder over their problems. People in poor countries living in conditions of constant conflict suffer from immense mental health problems. Usually there are no facilities to help them.

CARE IN THE COMMUNITY

In many countries, the only treatment for people with mental illness is to put them in an institution with other sufferers. Generally, little effective treatment is given there and patients do not get better. WHO is

A refugee from war-torn Kashmir. ▼

FACTFILE: Mental health

The civil war in Sri Lanka between 1983 and 2002 resulted in more than 64,000 deaths and shattered the economy. Thousands of people live in camps, having fled their homes because of the fighting. Their living conditions are terrible. The rate of suicide in the camps is almost three times higher than in the community in general. Sri Lanka as a country has one of the highest suicide rates in the world.

Source: *The Lancet*, UK, 2002

encouraging all countries to adopt a policy of caring for people in their own community. This means providing them with the treatment they need, for example, drugs and psychotherapy, and also adequate support from community health workers. Space in hospital should be available if people have a crisis and cannot cope at home.

WHO is also working to overcome the stigma in society attached to mental health problems. It spreads information, explaining that sufferers are not 'mad' and somehow separate from the rest of 'normal' society.

▲ A girl in Zambia receiving counselling to help her sort out her problems.

PROJECT ATLAS

It was realized by WHO that worldwide there was plenty of information about the burden of mental health problems on societies but little information about the

resources available to deal with them. In 2000, Project Atlas was launched. Details of the mental health resources of each country were compiled. These were put on the internet so that they would be easy to access and update. WHO hoped that the project would help to focus attention on mental health and lead to improved care for people who were suffering.

Chapter Five:
On the Frontline: Disease Control

ROLL BACK MALARIA

Malaria kills 1.1 million people a year in more than 30 countries. In 1998, WHO launched the Roll Back Malaria partnership, a global movement including UNICEF, UNDP (United Nations Development Programme), the World Bank, development agencies and many other organizations. In 1999, David Nabarro, project manager for Roll Back Malaria in WHO, announced that the number of treated mosquito bed nets provided for African children was to increase by thirty times over the following five years. Bed nets dipped in insecticide stop malaria-carrying mosquitoes from biting people at night.

'Dip-it-yourself' nets

Research work was done in Tanzania. The mosquito nets needed to be dipped in insecticide at least once or twice a year. There used to be 'dipping days', when people had to bring their nets to a centre to be dipped. But few people made the journey. It was decided that a 'dip-it-yourself' scheme would be better. Then people could dip the nets at home as part of their domestic washing routine.

Many Tanzanians do not read well, so it was vital to produce clear instructions for the kit with pictures as well as words. Experienced bed-net users helped to develop the kit. The instructions were tested among various groups of people in rural and urban communities by watching them using it. This was to make sure they used the kit safely and properly, avoiding waste.

A woman in Nigeria dipping a treated mosquito bed net in insecticide at home as part of the Roll Back Malaria scheme. ▶

> **"**The challenge of Olympic athletes is to take home medals. The challenge for many people is surviving malaria.**"**
>
> Fokasi Wilbroad Fullah,
> Tanzanian marathon runner
> and malaria survivor.

In 2001, Olympic athletes from Nigeria, Senegal, South Africa, Ethiopia and Tanzania pledged to help raise awareness about malaria and how best to prevent it. Among them were Ethiopian gold-medal-winning distance runners Haile Gebreselassie, Deratu Tulu and Fatuma Koba.

Saving children from malaria

The project has seen great success. Tanzanian companies started producing bed nets in large quantities. Taxes on the materials were removed, and the prices came down. In 2001, a single net cost US $2, which local people could afford. By that year, the insecticide-treated bed nets had reduced the death rate from malaria in children under 5 by 25 per cent in Tanzania in a community of 480,000. The country's goal is to protect 60 per cent of children and pregnant women with a treated bed net by 2005.

WHO is also working with the insecticide industry to produce new, improved insecticides for public health use. A new development is a long-lasting mosquito net that stays active for years, even when regularly washed. This will help further in the challenge to combat malaria.

Ethiopian gold-medal-winning athlete, Deratu Tulu, is helping to promote the Roll Back Malaria campaign. ▶

STOPPING TUBERCULOSIS

Tuberculosis (TB) is a deadly infectious disease. It kills around 3 million people a year worldwide and is spreading with frightening speed. When infectious people cough, sneeze, talk or spit, they release TB germs into the air that can infect other people. TB is particularly dangerous for people with weak immune systems and is the main cause of death among those infected with HIV.

TB is curable. But it is vital for people to complete their treatment. Where this does not happen, it can allow strains of TB that are resistant to drugs to develop. A key strategy for dealing with the disease is DOTS – Direct Observed Treatment Short-course. Patients are observed to make sure they take the drugs properly and complete the brief course of treatment.

▲ Many poverty-stricken TB sufferers, like this man, live on less than $10 a month.

FACTFILE: TB

- A single person with TB who is not treated can infect 10 to 15 other people each year.

    Source: Pan-American Health Organization, 2002

- Between 2000 and 2020 nearly 1 billion people will become infected with the TB bacterium. 200 million will develop the active disease and 35 million of them will die from TB – unless current treatment and prevention methods are improved.

    Source: NIAID Global Health Research Plan for HIV/AIDS, Malaria and TB, 2002

The case of Zimbabwe

Zimbabwe has six times more cases of TB than it did 20 years ago. The disease thrives in this country where AIDS is spreading like wildfire. One in four adults is infected with HIV. Poverty makes it worse; hungry people are more likely to catch TB because their bodies are too weak to resist the disease. In 2002, the economic crisis had left 80 per cent of the population living below the poverty line.

WHO is working with the Zimbabwean government to try to fight TB. The DOTS strategy was adopted in 1997. Anti-TB drugs are cheap, costing as little as US$10–$15 per person, and the government offers treatment free of charge. By 2002, about 25 per cent of TB patients were being observed during the intensive stage of the treatment.

Yet many patients still have no access to the drugs, which must be given daily by a health worker. WHO, the health ministry and NGOs have organized a campaign to provide information about TB in the worst-affected regions. The campaign is called 'Stop TB – fight poverty' because the two go hand in hand. However, without freely available, low-cost AIDS treatment as well, success in reducing TB cases may well be limited.

A TB patient in Ethiopia being given her treatment by a health worker as part of the DOTS scheme. ▼

"I was quite fortunate that the treatment for TB is free in this country. So I did not have to worry about funds for my health. I am now back at work and I do not have to worry about who will look after my brothers and sisters."

Fungai Mataya, a domestic worker in Harare, Zimbabwe, who has cared for her four younger brothers and sisters since their mother died of AIDS.

ERADICATING POLIO

Polio is a devastating disease that mostly affects children under five. Highly infectious, it invades the nervous system and causes total paralysis within hours. In 1 in 200 cases, the child is left paralysed for life, usually in the legs. No longer able to walk, he or she has to crawl or hobble on damaged legs. Of those paralysed, 5 to 10 per cent die. There is no cure; polio has to be prevented.

In 1988, the World Health Assembly launched a global initiative to eradicate polio by the end of 2000. By 2001, polio cases had decreased by 99.8 per cent since 1988, from an estimated 350,000 cases to 537. In 2002, Europe was declared polio free; there had not been a new case for three years.

◀ This teenage boy from Afghanistan has had polio and now has to walk on crutches. Immunization against polio is still low in a few countries, such as India and Pakistan.

FACTFILE:
Polio

- According to WHO, the last case of polio in Europe was in Turkey in 1998. A two-year-old boy who had not been immunized was paralysed by the virus.

- Before the campaign to eradicate polio about 1,000 children in the world were paralysed each day.

A polio-free world

The revised aim was to make the world polio-free by 2005. All children under five worldwide were to be immunized with the Oral Polio Vaccine (OPV). Any polio cases were to be reported. There would be targeted 'mop-up' campaigns in any area where polio was found. If a child caught polio, house-to-house visits would be made around the whole area to make sure all the local children were immunized.

DAYS OF TRANQUILLITY

It is quite a task to reach all children from densely populated urban areas to remote rural regions. A huge challenge is immunizing children caught up in conflict. To this end, WHO and its partners organize 'Days of Tranquillity'. Cease-fires are agreed to enable National Immunization Days to take place.

▲ Health workers in Yemen travel over mountains and through rivers to immunize children in remote areas.

The central African region is one of the last areas of the world where the wild polio virus is found. In summer 2001, the conflict-affected countries of Angola, Republic of Congo, the Democratic Republic of Congo and Gabon agreed to respect peace for several National Immunization Days. Tens of thousands of health workers and volunteers travelled around towns, cities, villages, border areas and refugee camps with the vaccine. More than 86,000 health workers delivered vaccines in the Democratic Republic of the Congo alone. Up to 16 million children received the polio vaccine.

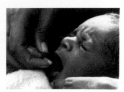

Chapter Six:
On the Frontline: Health Promotion

HIV/AIDS EDUCATION

As yet there is no cure for HIV/AIDS so the best policy is prevention. Worldwide, there is a huge level of ignorance about the disease. Millions do not know how to use simple methods to protect themselves.

The HIV virus is carried in the sexual fluids and blood of an infected person. If blood or sexual fluids get into the blood of another person, that person can become infected. The HIV virus is commonly spread between adults through sex. It can also be spread from mother to baby. HIV can be passed on by sharing equipment used to inject drugs. The best way to avoid becoming infected during sex is to use a condom.

Local NGO (Non-Governmental Organization) showing a video from a mobile van to raise awareness of contraception and condom use in Orissa, India. ▼

SAFER SEX

WHO, alongside partner organizations such as UNAIDS, has a key role to play in training health workers to educate people about safer sex practices. These organizations also try out and test training methods, and record best practice — what works best. These methods can then be adapted and used by other groups.

While HIV/AIDS is having a particularly devastating effect in developing countries, it remains a problem in developed countries too. In the USA, nearly half a million people were known to have the HIV virus or AIDS in 2001. UNAIDS has documented a project that was put into practice by high school teachers and students in Connecticut, USA. The programme helps to prevent HIV

Contrasting behaviour: a disapproving look as a young couple in China show their feelings. ▶

infection among first-year high school students (aged 14 and 15) in inner-city schools.

STUDENT EDUCATORS

First, the teachers deliver a four-day programme to the students. They show videos aimed at their age group, and appropriate to their culture. There are discussions and activities to encourage students' interest in HIV prevention. Then, the classes elect popular and respected students to be trained as peer counsellors. These students have training in how to lead discussions about HIV prevention with their classmates.

After the programme, it was found that students were more likely than those who hadn't been involved in the project to buy, carry and use condoms. The mixture of teacher-led and student-led activities was extremely effective.

ORGANIZATION IN FOCUS:
Working together

WHO co-operates with other United Nations agencies to improve world health. For example, it works with UNDP (see page 28), the United Nations Population Fund (UNFPA) and the World Bank on family planning and tropical diseases. WHO helps in emergencies, for example, aiding refugees alongside agencies such as the United Nations High Commission for Refugees (UNHCR).

NGOs are often critical of WHO over certain issues. For example, Médecins sans Frontières (Doctors without Borders), which campaigns for access to vital drugs for poor people, has criticized WHO for not doing enough to persuade the large pharmaceutical companies to reduce their prices (see page 17).

MATHARI – MODEL MENTAL HEALTH CARE

Lilian and Zachariah Kanaiya from Nairobi, Kenya, were proud of their son, Bacia. He was an outgoing 18-year-old, so they were surprised when he started refusing to go to school and lost interest in his friends. When they finally took him to a doctor, they found out Bacia had schizophrenia, a lifelong mental illness. At first Lilian and Zachariah denied their son was ill but eventually they accepted it and gave him their support. Lilian founded the Schizophrenia Foundation of Kenya to help others in a similar situation. Her efforts have now been recognized and publicized by WHO.

"Many times people who are mentally ill are associated with violence. You come to realize that this is just a stigma and something that society at large has decided.**"**

Gladys Okoth, whose son has schizophrenia, Kenya, 2001

Seen as stupid

In Kenya, the numbers with mental health illnesses are rising but the health system is completely inadequate. Generally, people with mental illnesses are seen as *wenda wazimu* – 'crazy fellows'. They suffer from discrimination, abuse and neglect. A person who has suffered a mental illness is assumed to be useless for ever.

Mathari Hospital – a success story

The only specialized mental health institution in Kenya is Mathari Psychiatric Hospital in Nairobi. As part of WHO's efforts to bring mental health issues to the top of the health agenda worldwide, the Director-General, Dr Gro Harlem Brundtland, visited Mathari on World Health Day in April 2001.

▼ Dr A. O. Onyango stands inside the newly-built Executive Psychiatric Wing of Mathari Hospital.

▲ Dr Onyango stands with nurses and patients outside the Psychiatric Wing of Mathari Hospital.

Mathari used to be like most mental health institutions around the world. Over 1,500 patients were crammed in, often staying for months or even years. There was no proper treatment and people were left with nothing to do. Nowadays there are around 400 patients. The average stay is just 14 days. Patients receive suitable drugs and other therapies that they need, such as psychotherapy. With the correct use of drugs and a good standard of care in the community, some patients do not even need to stay in the hospital at all.

The community approach

WHO officials working in the region with health experts have found that helping people in their communities really works. Teaching parents and health workers to spot mental health problems enables sufferers to be treated more quickly, before they become disabled by their illness. Nowadays, better drugs with fewer side effects are available too.

FACTFILE: Psychiatric help

According to WHO, in the African region, there are 1,200 psychiatrists and 12,000 psychiatric nurses serving a population of 620 million people (in other words, there are 2 psychiatrists and 20 nurses per million people). In contrast, in the European region, which includes the countries of the former Soviet Union, there are 86,000 psychiatrists and 280,000 nurses serving a population of 870 million (or 99 psychiatrists and 320 nurses per million people).

◀ The Paralympic Games of 2000 was a tobacco-free event. Since the late 1980s, the Olympic movement has been tobacco free, with smoking not permitted at most venues.

TOBACCO FREE SPORT

An important part of WHO's TFI is the Tobacco Free Sport campaign, which aims to rid sport of all association with tobacco. The tobacco industry spends millions of pounds each year sponsoring sports. Tobacco companies like to associate their deadly product with healthy activities. The Tobacco Free Sport campaign aims to destroy this link and to encourage people to be involved in sport but not to smoke.

Saying no to tobacco sponsorship

FIFA, the world football governing body, has refused to allow tobacco sponsorship at its events since 1987. In 2002, the World Cup kick-off was on World No Tobacco Day. This was a great opportunity for WHO to publicize the dangers of smoking.

Some people have argued that sports organizations will have money problems if they do not accept sponsorship from tobacco companies. Yet football enjoyed great financial success in the 1990s after kicking tobacco out of the stadiums.

THE EVILS OF SMOKING

Around the world, millions of people buy a product that has no health benefits and can cause terrible harm and even death – tobacco. Yet it continues to be produced, advertised and sold. The WHO Tobacco Free Initiative (TFI) is a worldwide campaign against smoking.

Tobacco sponsorship in Malaysia

The Tobacco Free Initiative has led to the Olympics being tobacco free, which is a great success for WHO. However, it has not yet been effective in stopping tobacco companies from getting around the rules. For example, in Malaysia, there are strict controls on tobacco advertising. Sponsorship of sport is used as a way round the regulations. The British American Tobacco (BAT) brand Dunhill sponsors the domestic football league and the national soccer team. During the 2002 World Cup, declared tobacco free by FIFA, BAT sponsored the television coverage of the World Cup matches to promote Dunhill cigarettes. BAT branding appeared in newspapers and on Malaysian TV. Anti-smoking campaigners considered this a highly irresponsible act. Working out how to deal with sponsorship of sport by tobacco companies still presents a challenge for WHO.

> **"**This World Cup is different from other World Cups as FIFA has tied it up to World No Tobacco Day with the theme of tobacco-free sports. This is a cruel joke to Malaysia as BAT is bombarding the nation with adverts of Dunhill's sponsorship of the World Cup … We cannot enjoy tobacco-free football. This is highly irresponsible and the management in both Britain and Malaysia should be ashamed.**"**
>
> Mary Assunta of the Consumers' Association of Penang, Malaysia, 2002 World Cup

◄ Soccer star David Beckham signs autographs for Malaysian fans. In Malaysia, Dunhill sponsors the television coverage of the English Premier League, which is very popular there.

WHO has had some great successes since its establishment in 1948. Yaws, a disease that caused disfigurement (spoiled people's appearance) and disability, was one of the first diseases tackled by the organization. In 1948, a single penicillin injection was introduced that could cure it once and for all.

Onchocerciasis is being successfully tackled by spraying around rivers to kill the blackflies that carry the disease. About 10 million children born in the eleven West African countries targeted since the programme began are no longer at risk of catching it. ▼

ERADICATING DISEASES

A major milestone was the successful eradication of smallpox. In 1967, between 10 and 15 million people were struck with the disease. Some 2 million of them died and millions of others were blinded or scarred for life. Smallpox was officially declared eradicated in 1980. If it hadn't been wiped out, at least 20 million people would have died from it over the following twenty years. Polio was eradicated in Europe in 2002. It is hoped the world will be polio free by the year 2005.

Fighting leprosy and guinea-worm disease

There are six countries where leprosy is still a big problem: Brazil, India, Madagascar, Mozambique, Myanmar and Nepal. With WHO's help, these countries are stepping up their efforts to wipe out the disease. Guinea-worm disease is found in tropical African and Asian countries. Caused by a worm that buries under the skin, it is caught from drinking impure water. It creates dreadful suffering and disability among some of the poorest people in sub-Saharan Africa. WHO has promoted simple measures to protect against it, such as filtering water. In 2002, over 36,800 cases were reported to WHO, compared with over 54,000 cases in the previous year.

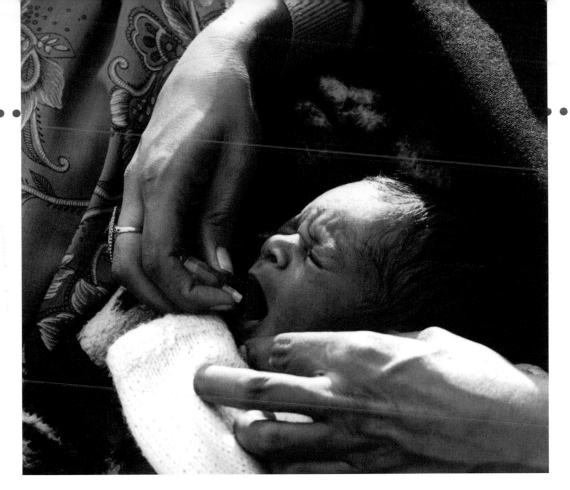

Success of immunization

Millions of children have been saved from disability and death from infectious diseases through WHO's immunization programme. Eight out of ten children in the world today are protected from six major childhood diseases: polio, measles, diphtheria, whooping cough, tetanus and tuberculosis.

WHO has also helped countries to improve their health services and reduce death rates. It has helped to deliver essential drugs, often at reduced prices. The organization has brought in guidelines to assist in the creation of healthier cities. WHO's work has contributed to a healthier world.

▲ A baby being immunized against polio in a New Delhi street in India. WHO hopes polio will be eradicated within a few years.

FACTFILE: Disease prevention

In 2000, 3 million children were able to survive who would have died from preventable diseases in 1990.

Source: *The Guardian*/Save the Children, *Taking Children Seriously*, 2002

An old people's home in Bolivia. No longer living as they used to, in extended families, many elderly people now have to be cared for in institutions.

CHALLENGES FOR WHO

WHO faces a number of challenges. World population is increasing, as is the proportion of elderly people, with their great need for health care. Non-communicable diseases such as heart disease, cancer and mental illness are growing at an alarming rate. The gap between rich and poor countries and inequality within nations is continuing to widen. This means a growing health divide between wealthier, healthier people and poor people who suffer more from disease.

FACTFILE: Population growth and the ageing population

- Since 1950, the global population has more than doubled. By late 1999 it had reached 6 billion. It will increase by nearly 80 million people a year to reach about 8 billion by the year 2025.

- In 2002, one in 10 people was aged 60 or over. By 2020, this figure is expected to be one in eight. Of all the world's elderly people, two-thirds live in developing countries.

- Globally, the population of children under 5 will grow by just 0.25% annually between 2002 and 2025. The population over 65 years will grow by 2.6%.

- Average life expectancy at birth in 1955 was just 48 years. In 1995 it was 65 years. In 2025 it will reach 73 years. But in 1998, more than 50 million people lived in countries with a life expectancy of less than 45 years.

Source: WHO

Pressure from NGOs

Many NGOs argue that WHO could be doing more to encourage the development of drugs to help the world's poor. They want WHO to be more courageous in persuading the big pharmaceutical companies to lower the prices of essential drugs sold to poor countries. Oxfam has called for developing countries to have the right to obtain the cheapest possible life-saving medicines.

The need for new drugs

In 2001, the international medical aid agency Médecins sans Frontières (MSF) reported that from 11 of the largest pharmaceutical companies in the world, only one new TB drug had been brought to the market in the previous five years. It is crucial to develop new drugs because TB strains are developing that are resistant to the treatment available.

"Drugs are not developed according to public health need, but according to profitability."

Dr Bernard Pécoul, Director of MSF's Campaign for Access to Essential Medicines, 2001

'Neglected diseases'

An MSF director, Bernard Pécoul, has pointed to 'neglected diseases' such as Chagas' disease (a disease caused by blood-sucking bugs) and leishmaniasis (a disease caused by sandflies). These diseases, which mainly affect poor people, were supposed to be wiped out by 2000. It didn't happen. Pécoul criticized WHO for not putting pressure on the pharmaceutical industry to develop treatments for them.

The AIDS crisis remains far from over. Infection rates are still soaring and there is no cure available. The drugs that can keep people alive are too costly for poor countries, putting them out of the reach of the majority of AIDS sufferers. There is still a long way to go to achieve WHO's aim of health for all.

◀ Laboratory workers carrying out research into malaria. Out of the 1,393 new drugs approved between 1975 and 1999, only 13 (1 per cent) were for tropical diseases. Yet tropical diseases such as malaria affect millions of people every year.

LOOKING TO THE FUTURE

There are fantastic opportunities for new technology to improve health. Knowledge about how our genes work has led to the possibility of gene therapy. This will hopefully be able to cure people with a genetic disease, such as cystic fibrosis, by altering the faulty gene. Research has shown that stem cells, for example from the umbilical cord of a newborn baby, could be used to develop treatments for diseases that can't be cured at the moment. It seems likely that human beings could be cloned to create spare organs that could be used as replacements for ones that fail. But all these developments need to be handled carefully to make sure that people's rights are always respected. WHO leads discussions on the social and ethical issues of gene technology.

Worrying prospects

The world is faced with environmental problems. Our natural resources are being used up. Toxic chemicals are pumped out by factories and vehicles, and are used in farming to produce our food. High levels of pollution may cause more heart and lung disease. Due to the process of global warming, more regions are suffering from flooding as well as higher temperatures. A warmer, wetter environment allows mosquitoes to multiply, spreading malaria. This presents new challenges for WHO's Roll Back Malaria programme.

The world is full of conflict. WHO has to consider the possible use of chemical and biological weapons, or even nuclear weapons. The mass destruction these could cause would present a huge challenge to WHO and other health organizations.

THE CHALLENGE FOR WHO

Urgent action is required to tackle the diseases that most threaten human health. Unless the spread of AIDS is halted, there will be 70 million deaths from the disease over the next 20 years. Without addressing this

This boy has been treated for sickle-cell disease, a painful blood disorder. It is hoped that some day gene therapy will cure this inherited disease. ▼

problem, many countries in Africa, and increasingly elsewhere, will simply not be able to develop. A healthy population is necessary for a country to grow economically.

Reducing poverty is essential to improving people's health. Weak, underfed people are likely to fall ill. But inequality and poverty remain

▲ People at this farming co-operative in Rwanda work together to earn a living.

some of the biggest problems in the world. This is perhaps the main reason why delivering its global policy 'Health for All' is such an enormous challenge for WHO.

ORGANIZATION IN FOCUS:
Health for All in the 21st Century

Health for All in the 21st Century – WHO's new global health policy

- The enjoyment of good health is the fundamental right of every human being.

- It is necessary to reduce social and economic inequality to improve everyone's health. Therefore, WHO should pay most attention to those with the greatest needs.

- Health systems should be strengthened and should provide health services for everyone.

- We need to work together as a community of nations.

antibodies Substances that the body produces in order to fight disease.

BSE (bovine spongiform encephalopathy) A usually fatal disease of cattle, which can be passed on to humans in the form of Creutzfeldt-Jakob disease, also fatal.

cholera A dangerous infectious disease causing severe vomiting and diarrhoea.

communicable diseases Diseases that can be passed from one person to another.

convention An official agreement between countries or leaders.

developed world The parts of the world, including Europe, the USA and Australia, where there are many industries and a complex economic system.

developing countries The poorer countries that are trying to advance their industries and economic system.

development agencies Organizations that work in poor countries to help people to develop their industries and economy and improve their lives.

epidemic A widespread outbreak of disease in a community.

eradicate To wipe out completely.

global warming The increase in temperature of the Earth's atmosphere, caused by the increase of particular gases, especially carbon dioxide.

immune system The system in your body that produces substances to help it to fight against infection and disease.

immunization The protection of people against disease, usually by giving them a vaccine.

insecticide A chemical used for killing insects.

larvae (singular: larva) Insects at the stage when they have just come out of the egg and look like a little worm.

life expectancy The number of years a person is likely to live.

malnutrition A condition that comes from having a poor or inadequate diet.

maternal Of mothers.

multi-drug therapy (MDT) A treatment using a combination of different drugs.

non-communicable diseases Diseases that cannot be caught from another person.

non-governmental organization (NGO) A charity or association that is independent from government or business.

obesity Being so fat that it is bad for the person's health.

paralysis The loss of control and sometimes feeling in a part of the body.

parasite A tiny animal or plant that lives inside another animal or plant and gets its food from it. The malaria parasite lives on humans.

pharmaceutical To do with making and selling drugs and medicines.

psychiatric To do with mental illness. A psychiatric hospital is a place where mental illnesses are treated.

psychotherapy The treatment of mental illness by discussing a person's problems with him or her rather than giving drugs.

sanitation The system that keeps places clean, especially by removing human waste.

schizophrenia A mental illness that makes people out of touch with reality for at least some of the time.

side effect An extra and usually bad effect that a drug has on a person.

smallpox A serious infectious disease that causes fever, leaves permanent skin damage and often kills.

sponsorship The giving of money by a company to help pay for an event, for example, a sports contest, in return for allowing the company to advertise its products at the event.

stem cells Basic cells from which all other kinds of cells develop to make up the different parts of the body.

toxic Poisonous.

transnational Operating in many different countries.

UNDP United Nations Development Programme

UNICEF The United Nations Children's Fund

vaccine A substance that is put into the blood, usually through an injection, to protect the person from disease.

virus A tiny living thing that causes infectious disease in people, animals or plants.

World Bank An agency of the United Nations that promotes the economic development of countries. It encourages private companies to invest in development projects and lends money to countries from its own funds.

yaws An infectious tropical skin disease, causing large red swellings.

FURTHER READING

Great Inventions: Medicine, Paul Dowswell, Heinemann, 2001.
Health issues: AIDS, Jo Whelan, Hodder Wayland, 2001.
Health issues: Smoking, Sally Morgan, Hodder Wayland, 2001.
Health and Medicine, Jane Shuter, Heinemann, 2000.
World Health, Ronan Foley, Hodder Wayland, 2002.
World Organizations: World Health Organization, Jillian Powell, Franklin Watts, 2000.

USEFUL ADDRESSES

Médecins Sans Frontières
Rue de la Tourelle 39
Brussels
Belgium
www.msf.org

Save the Children Fund (UK)
17 Grove Lane
London
SE5 8RD
www.savethechildren.org.uk

Save the Children Fund (USA)
54 Wilton Road
Westport, CT 06880
www.savethechildren.org

World Health Organization (Headquarters)
20 Avenue Appia
1211 Geneva 27
Switzerland
www.who.int/

alcohol 14, 26
Argentina 23

Bolivia 17, 24, 42
Botswana 18, 19
Brazil 19, 40
breastfeeding 25
Britain 11, 14, 15
Brundtland, Gro Harlem 11, 15, 37

campaigns
  anti-smoking 38–9
  health education 22–3, 34–5
  HIV/AIDS 9, 18, 19, 34–5
  immunization 8–9, 16–17, 32–3, 41
  malaria 28–9
  pregnancy and childbirth 24–5
child death rates 13, 21, 25, 29, 41
conflicts 26, 27, 33, 44
Congo 8, 33

'Days of Tranquillity' 33
diarrhoea 12
diseases
  BSE 14, 15
  Chagas' disease 43
  cholera 5, 6
  Ebola 4–5
  guinea-worm disease 40
  hepatitis B 16
  HIV/AIDS 9, 18–19, 24, 25, 30, 31, 34–5, 43, 44–5
  leishmaniasis 43
  leprosy 20, 40
  malaria 12, 15, 21, 25, 28–9, 43, 44
  non-communicable 14, 15, 42
  polio 8, 9, 32–3, 40, 41
  river blindness (onchocerciasis) 20–21, 40
  smallpox 6, 8, 9, 40
  tuberculosis (TB) 8, 30–31, 41, 43
  yaws 9, 40

'DOTS' scheme 30, 31
drugs
  cost of 12, 13, 15, 16–17, 18–19, 20, 21, 31, 35, 43
  disease resistance 21, 30
  generic 19
  research and development 13, 15, 17, 18, 45

elderly people 42
emergency response 4–5, 10, 11, 35
environmental problems 14, 23, 43
Europe 6, 9, 11, 14, 32, 37

food safety 14, 15

gene therapy 44
Global Outreach Alert and Response Network 4, 5

healthy eating 22

India 6, 19, 24, 32, 40, 41

Kenya 36–7

life expectancy 13, 42

Malaysia 39
malnutrition 23, 25
Médecins sans Frontières 13, 35, 43
mental health issues
  community health care 27, 37
  Project Atlas 27
mosquito nets 28–9

Niger 12
Nigeria 11, 28
non-governmental organizations (NGOs) 11, 31, 35, 43

obesity 14, 15
Onchocerciasis Control Programme 20–21, 40

patents 17, 19
pharmaceutical companies 13, 15, 16–17, 18, 19, 20, 21, 35, 43
pollution 14, 23, 44
population growth 42
poverty 12, 13, 16, 18–19, 23, 24, 25, 30, 31, 40, 42, 43, 45

rehydration salts 12
Roll Back Malaria 28–9, 44

sanitation 5, 6, 7, 13
smoking 14, 15, 26, 38–9
Sri Lanka 27
sun protection 22

Tanzania 28–9
Tobacco Free Initiative 38–9
training programmes 9, 34
TRIPS agreement 17, 19

Uganda 4–5
UNAIDS 9, 18, 19, 34–5
UNICEF 9, 25, 28
United Nations 7, 11
USA 11, 34–5

vaccines 8, 9, 11, 13, 16–17, 33

water supplies 5, 6, 12, 13, 23, 40
WHO
  aims 7
  budget 10
  establishment of 7
  funding 11
  headquarters 4
  links with other agencies 4, 5, 9, 11, 20, 28, 35
  structure 10
  task forces 5
World Bank 11, 20, 28, 35
World Health Assembly 7, 10, 22, 32

Zimbabwe 31